I0182839

Principles
and Issues

> The Rules of Reality
> The Laws of Thought

From Why We Shouldn't Call Our Ancestors Slaves

Copyright © (2025) by (LaRue Nedd, BLD)

Published by FNNC Publishing

ISBN: 978-0-9856896-5-0

PRINCIPLES & ISSUES
Rules of Reality and Thought

PRINCIPLES & ISSUES
Rules of Reality and Thought

Contents:

PRINCIPLES & ISSUES
Rules of Reality and Thought

PRINCIPLES AND ISSUES

As A Man Thinketh

The aphorism, "as a man thinketh in his heart so is he," not only embraces the whole of a man's being, but is so comprehensive as to reach out to every condition and circumstance of his life. A man is literally what he thinks, his character being the complete sum of all his thoughts...

As the plant springs from, and could not be without the seed, so every act of a man springs from the hidden seeds of thought and could not have appeared without them. This applies equally to those acts called "spontaneous" and "unpremeditated" as to those which are deliberately executed.[1]

As A Man Thinketh
By James Allen

The Formula

The formula, *therefore, is that common beliefs and thoughts produce common actions that produce common results in a common environment every time.*

And one of the most damaging beliefs that Black American African people have about Black American African people is that we are the descendants of a people who were slaves to White people. The word slave when applied to Black people in slavery has a different meaning as compared to other people, times, conditions, and situations.

In the end, all that any of us want to do is to live and enjoy life. If we have children, we want to see them do the same thing. Sometimes, we automatically feel good when we can help other people. Sometimes when we help other people, we help ourselves.

According to our actions in our communities and our expressions, through music, art, and writing, it seems that most of us are living in hell on Earth instead of heaven on Earth. If you judge a tree by the fruit it produces, it does not look like the Black American African people are a happy people; and according to the statistics and what we can see, it shows in every area of our society. It shows in our music, our art, and our thinking. Just because we smile, laugh, and party; it does not mean that we are happy and enjoying life in general.

The Problem

The question is, do Black people need self-help books specifically written for the Black American African people. One of the reasons why most self-help books fail Black people is that they do not get to the root of the problem. They do not take our history, our environment, and our situation as a people into consideration. If we are not trying to solve the problems that divide our house, then what matters?

They analyze and diagnose our problems as if the effects of slavery have dissipated. However, the fact is that many of the changes that were imposed on us, as a people, during slavery are still with us to this day. They think and act as if Black people's problems and White people's (other people's) problems are the same and work the same way because we are all human beings. Although there are similarities, there are also differences. There are differences in our genetics, our spirituality, and our histories. Therefore, the dynamics of our problems are not the same as they are for other people.

One difference is obvious. When you look at the problems in American society, in every area, we suffer more. The Foster Childcare System is full of our children. Self-destructive behavior, heinous and nonsensical crimes, shootings, and homicide rates are epidemic in Black communities across America. We see high rates of alcohol, drug, and sexual abuse.

And, although it is not considered to be a crime, **the most devastating problem** that Black people face is the **division that exists in our families.** In fact, there is so much division in our families and communities that we now see it as being normal.

One parent cannot do what two parents can do. Two parents cannot do what an extended family can do. When grandma and grandpa are not present, much knowledge and wisdom is lost. The breakup and dysfunction of our families tends to stunt the mental and spiritual growth of our children and prevents them from being competitive with others who come from healthy functional families.

These problems are not restricted to poor Black people. As adults, one way or another, the vast majority of us are caught-up in a battle for self-control. Too many of us are in a self-destructive mode and do not understand why.

The aim of this book is to help improve the quality of life for Black people by providing information that will help improve the way we see ourselves which will automatically influence the way we act toward each other. From the time we were brought here to be "slaves," which was not that long ago, the status and mental condition of Black people have always been in question even by Black people. Therefore, in the introduction of Tom Burrell's book, *Brainwashed,* he asks:

> So then why, after all this time, when calculating the achievement of the "American Dream," are we still ranked at the bottom of almost every "good" list, and at the top of the "bad" lists? Why, despite our apparent strength, intelligence, and resourcefulness, do we continue to lag behind and languish in so many aspects of American life?[2]

The subtitle of his book is, "**Challenging the Myth of Black Inferiority**." And that is exactly what this book is doing as well. All myths about Black inferiority are rooted in the idea that our ancestors were slaves to the Europeans and that we lived like savages in Africa before we were brought here.

If a person was kidnapped at a young age and put in an environment where everyone including the church, the school, and the news media told them that they were inferior; after a time, they would begin to believe it. The belief that Black people are inferior is the legacy of slavery.

PRINCIPLES & ISSUES
Rules of Reality and Thought

We may not admit it openly, but many of us believe it. The proof shows in our standards of beauty, our words, and our actions as a people. If we look closely at the pandemic problems that exist amongst us as a people, it would not be difficult to see that many of these problems are related to self-esteem issues. They are directly related to how we view and value ourselves as a people.

Some of us have even been convinced that something is intrinsically wrong with Black people. They believe that we are inferior by Nature or GOD's will and that slavery took us out of savagery. They also believe that Euro-American cultures and religions are universally correct. They reject their African identity and culture. Therefore, the only reason they call themselves Black or African American is because they seem to have no choice.

Believing that our ancestors were slaves influences our understanding of who we are and what we do. If we believe that our ancestors were slaves, then we must also believe that we are the descendants of slaves. And, in believing so, we will act accordingly. One major theme of this book is that we act according to what we think we are.

I am not saying that **"slavery"** did not exist. I am saying that the word **slave** does not and should not be applied to the ancestors of Black American Africans or any Black people. Some people believe that if we did not call them slaves it would diminish our understanding of slavery and its impact.

In truth, our understanding of our history is further diminished by calling our ancestors slaves because it tends to move us to not look at our history. It prompts us to avoid studying our history from our point of view. What is the difference between a prisoner, a hostage, a captive, and a slave?

Many books, movies, and documentaries have been and still are being made about the physical aspects of slavery. At the same time, there is a mental and spiritual side to slavery. It is probably **the most studied subject in American history.** In addition, slavery and colonialism have had the greatest influence on African people in modern times. Therefore, it deserves our attention.

However, the more we look at the effect of calling and believing that our ancestors were slaves the more we will see the importance of this issue. This is especially true when it is coupled with the other negative propaganda about Black people. Although some of us have rejected the idea that our ancestors were slaves, understanding the reasons and the effects of calling them slaves needs to be explored. It is the lynch pin that allows all the other negative propaganda to be accepted as true.

Does calling our ancestors slaves have an effect on how we see ourselves? Does it affect our ability to think clearly and logically? Does it affect our ability to prosper in an environment that has a long history of oppressing Black people? Every self-help book ever written, including the Bible, tells us that there is a direct relationship between our thoughts, beliefs, actions, and the results we get. Therefore, how do our thoughts about our origins, our ancestry and our history affect us?

Many social programs, books and speeches have tried to raise the consciousness and quality of life for Black people. Still, the disparity widens because we have not gotten to the root of the problem. The success rates of these programs would be much higher if we had a more positive understanding of where we came from, our true Spirit and Nature, and our situation.

This is true because we act on what we see; and what we see is influenced, filtered, and colored by what we believe about ourselves. And our beliefs about our identity are central to what we do and the results we get. There is a connection between what a person thinks or does not think about their race and what they think about who they are as a member of that race or group of people.

In examining the problems that plague Black communities across this country, we can see that the majority of our problems are related to our self-concept, our ego, and our self-esteem which is rooted in our beliefs and understanding of Black people.

All Are Affected

All Black people, rich and poor, are in the same American boat. Calling our ancestors slaves affects the esteem of all Black people because it speaks about the quality of our nature by way of the people from whom we descended. Money does not heal these problems. In some cases, money may even make them worse because of what people must go through to get the money. Money also gives people more power to act on the negative thoughts that possess them.

Even White people are affected. Some feel guilty about the way their ancestors treated Black people. Some feel superior (a feeling of White supremacy) because of the power and privilege that they have inherited from their ancestors. Some suffer from **cognitive dissonance**, a feeling of conflicting beliefs, values, and attitudes. And because of this, they want to squash the subject and keep us from thinking about it.

The belief that our ancestors were slaves was implanted in all of us at an early age. And, because it relates to the people from whom we descended, it is impossible for this belief to not have an effect on all Black American Africans. From the Black American African activist to those who are well educated in African culture and customs to those who know very little about African or American African history, all have been affected by the belief that our Ancestors were slaves.

If you believe it, you are directly affected. If you do not believe it, you are indirectly affected by the people you know that do believe it. If it has an effect on our children, it has an effect on us. Therefore, there are no Black people who have not been affected by the belief that our ancestors were slaves.

All of us know that there is nothing good or positive about being a slave or being called a slave especially in the context of American and European history. Many of us think that we must accept this belief because it is true. Therefore, it is important that we examine the definition and the truthfulness and the effects of calling our ancestors slaves. The word "slave" is a negative word. If we apply it to our ancestors, the people from whom we descended, we also apply it to ourselves. What is the difference between a hostage, a prisoner, a captive, and a slave?

The First Time

Imagine how our children feel when they are bused into schools where they are the minority. Imagine them sitting in a classroom and being one of two or three Black children out of twenty or more White children in the class. Then, imagine how they feel when they begin to learn about American history.

American history is full of examples of how Europeans came to America, conquered the land and the people, and overcame all other types of adversity. They give credit for their triumphs to their spirit as a people. At the same time, our children are taught that the Black African people were slaves to the Euro-American people. At that point, what could possibly be going through our children's minds?

In the late 1960's, when I was very young, I use to get up every Saturday morning to watch Tarzan on TV. That was about the only time Black people could be seen on television. I tried to look behind Tarzan to see what the Africans were doing because they looked like me. However, they were too far in the background and all I could get was a glimpse. Still, every Saturday I hoped I would get a chance to learn a little more about Black people and my heritage.

In those days, one of the worst things a person could call you was a "black dog". The word black was more painful than the word dog. At the same time, if you told someone to do something that they did not want to do, they would respond with, **"I ain't your slave."** Being a slave was considered to be as bad as or worse than being a black dog.

In the mid 1960's, Black people were starved for positive social and cultural recognition, and we still are to this day. That is why I got excited when I learned that we were going to learn about Black people's history in our Social Studies period. I was ready to learn. Then, the first thing the teacher showed us in the book was that Black people were slaves to White people. I was disappointed again. Being dark skinned was bad enough and being the descendant of slaves seemed like a double blow to me.

Do you remember how you felt the first time you learned you were a descendant of slaves? What did you think? How did you feel? If you did not feel anything, it had to be because you had already been numbed by the system. Today, our children are much more aware of things than we were at their age. What are they learning about their history, their ancestors, and who they are? What are they thinking? Do they even care?

Roots

When Alex Haley's mini-series "Roots" came on TV in the late 1970's, the masses of Black people were very eager to learn about Black history during slavery (so were White people). We thought we were going to learn the truth about slavery. In addition, we were starving for social recognition as a people. We thought that Roots would be something good for us to watch.

PRINCIPLES & ISSUES
Rules of Reality and Thought

The series ran every day for one week, and it seemed that everyone I knew was highly motivated to watch it. Almost every well-known Black actor was in it. It was an epic event. When it was over, almost everyone believed that that was the way it was. We had seen enough.

Roots and all other movies about slavery have mixed lies and truth into one picture. They depict Black people in an inferior status to White people. They imply that White people (other people) control our freedom. They imply that most of us had accepted our fate and that only a few individuals fought back, if any. Therefore, we believe that our ancestors who were in slavery were slaves.

Today, the **propaganda** machine is even more pervasive and effective in mis-educating us about us and projecting negative images of Black people. Their messages are subtle and subliminal. Almost every Black American African activist recognizes that the images being projected today are only updated versions of those projected during slavery and the Jim Crow era.

If we accept these negative images as the whole truth, we will act accordingly, making what we believe come true. Then, they become self-fulfilling beliefs. As a result, believing in these negative images helps to support our disproportionate suffering in the land of plenty. Because we have been bombarded with information that says our ancestors were slaves, it is not enough just to say that our ancestors were not slaves. We must understand the logic and the effect that the word slave has on the psyche of Black people. Our children must know that our ancestors were not slaves and that they are not the descendants of slaves.

No healing can take place until the illness is acknowledged and understood.

THE PRINCIPLES AND ISSUES

What is in a name? Does the belief that our ancestors were slaves influence our identity and how we see ourselves? Exactly what do we mean when we call our ancestors slaves? If names have no meaning or effect, then what difference does it make what we call our ancestors or ourselves? If it does not matter, then why insist on calling them slaves?

I think that most people believe that the names we apply to ourselves are very important. Therefore, one of the biggest debates in the Black community is over the use of the "N" word. The fact that we call it the "N word" and the debate itself implies the importance of the names we use to identify ourselves as individuals and as a people.

The Principles of Thought

Just like everything else in the Universe and the world, our thoughts and beliefs work according to universal laws and order. The same laws that govern cause and effect also govern thoughts, beliefs, actions and their results.

All of our feelings and actions are the product of thought. Since this book is about correcting the error of calling the ancestors of Black American Africans slaves and other negative thoughts and beliefs about Black people, it is necessary for us to examine some basic laws of how thoughts and beliefs work and where they come from.

Lack of knowledge and understanding are at the root of all suffering. Having knowledge and understanding leads to happiness and healing. When we understand the principles or laws that govern the Universe and our world, it can only lead to our growth, development, and happiness. They can only improve the quality of our lives.

If we're not aware of these laws our thinking will be subject to error. We will be more likely to fall into **traps**. We will not be in harmony with the Universe. We will not see reality as it is. We will be confused about what is possible and what is not possible. These laws are core knowledge that are the solid foundation for wisdom and understanding. The more we are in harmony with these laws, the more we will be in harmony with the Universe and the self.

If the **foundation** is not solid, that which is built on it will be subject to collapse, error, and will not stand the test of time. If we don't understand the rules of the road, we will most likely conform to a law or laws that will not be to our benefit or will even be harmful to us.

Some Universal Laws

Because Universal laws are not physical, all Universal laws occupy or exist in the same space and time at the same time. They are infinite and everywhere. Universal laws do not change and cannot be changed. They are the rules of GOD. Under specific conditions, they will produce specific results every time.

PRINCIPLES & ISSUES
Rules of Reality and Thought

From Nothing, Nothing Comes:

This Law can be viewed from different angles such as you cannot get something from nothing. You cannot turn something into nothing. Nothing is no thing. Nothing means no time, no space, no darkness, no light, no any thing. Even in our imagination we cannot picture no-thing. To the contrary, this means that there is always something. This means that there is something that is infinite, always was and always will be.

Related to this law are: From like, like comes. From life, life comes. This same law is recognized in the Bible in Genesis when it says that everything was created after its own kind. And during the process of creation, not one kind of anything was created, not one kind of Light, not one kind of water, not one kind of dirt, grass, etc. And this applies to all animals including mankind.

However, if you can get people to believe the impossible is possible, you can get them to believe almost anything. And there are some things that are impossible such as getting something from nothing. This is a core belief that many other beliefs are built on or rooted in. if we can believe that we can get something from nothing, our logical thought processes will be distorted.

The Law of Opposites:

Everything (other than GOD) has an opposite. Everything has a positive and negative side. There is good and bad in everything and there is positive and negative in everything. That which is good for the farmer may not be good for the farm animals in the long run.

The Law of vibration:

The entire Universe is a vibration. Everything in the universe vibrates and has its own distinct vibration, every color, every chemical, even our thoughts and beliefs. This law works in union with ALL other universal laws. In the Universe there are an infinite number of vibrations.

At the same time, there are two basic types of vibrations one is peace and harmony, and the other is violent and destructive. One brings things together and the other drives things away or apart. One is constructive and the other is destructive relatively speaking. They are opposite sides of the same coin. It is the process that causes change by laws that do not change.

The law of vibrations is based on the binary code of the Universe. Even as babies we were born understanding the universal language of these two basic vibrations. Babies move us by smiling, laughing, and crying. Good vibrations and bad vibrations are the driving force of the Drum Major Instinct and the sex drive and mostly behind everything we do.

Music teaches us about the power of vibrations and words and is a vital part of every culture. Sometimes we can't see or hear vibrations, but we say, "I just had a feeling." Therefore, it is important for us to understand the law of vibrations and our individual vibration. From the whole Universe to the tiny individual person and blade of grass, each has a particular vibration. And this law is directly related to the law of specifics.

However, pleasure is the bait of many traps and can even lead to self-destruction. Therefore, there are other laws that must be taken into consideration such as the laws of cause and effect. Everything that feels good or tastes good may not be good for you. And this is the test where only the strong survive.

The Law of Cause and Effect:

($E=mc^2$). Everything has a cause and an effect. It is related to the laws of action. Certain actions will produce particular effects under certain conditions. It is related to the law of specifics. Every detective, every scientist, and all religions believe and teach a process of cause and effect. They believe that if they do the right thing they will get the right result.

We can see how the law of cause and effect relates to when things touch each other they influence each other. We can see how it relates to the metaphor we reap what we sow. You get out of life, what you put into life. Because our knowledge and wisdom are limited, we may not fully understand what we are sowing. And this is why we should allow what we think we know and what we believe to be reviewed and reviewed again.

The Law of Attraction

The Law of Attraction states that positive energies will always attract positive energies while negative energies will always attract negative energies. The paradox is that there are positive and negatives in everything. Things that are alike attract; opposites repel. Some people believe that opposites attract. They use the analogy of a magnet to prove their point. However, what they do not see is the flow of magnetic energy. The flow of energy is what attracts or repels magnets.

By the law of attraction, we tend to hang around people who are more like us, who think like us, and have similar mental and spiritual needs. Most likely, these people will have a common culture, heritage, history and personal experiences. Even in our personal relationships, it is the things that we agree on that bring us together and the things that we disagree about that drive us apart. By the law of attraction, we are attracted to places, things, and people according to our thoughts, beliefs, and vibrations. It is related to the law of cause and effect.

The Law of Specifics

A tree cannot just be a tree. It must be a specific kind of tree. And there are no two trees that are exactly alike. This same principle applies to all physical things. The same applies to human beings. A human being cannot simply be human. A person must be a specific kind of human. Race and sex are important parts of individual human existence. We could not exist without them.

The Law of Love

"He who knows nothing, loves nothing. He who can do nothing understands nothing. He who understands nothing is worthless.

But he who understands also loves, notices, sees ... The more knowledge is inherent in a thing, the greater the love.... Anyone who imagines that all fruits ripen at the same time as the strawberries knows nothing about grapes."

> *--Paracelsus*
> *Goodreads, Quotable Quotes*

Like everything else in the Universe, love has its laws. Although it may have many applications, it has its particular order and process. It is directly related to the law of learning. The most important things that we can apply it to are GOD, God, and self. There is no scripture in any culture that tells people that they should not love themselves or their God.

Since we cannot give what we do not have, we must get it before we can share it. This is where the principle of ask, seek, and knock comes into play. It works every time. It works according to the law of attraction. We cannot depend on a system that put us in slavery, that was built on slavery to free us. There is a reason why we are still at the bottom of the good list and the top of the bad list.

Thoughts to Actions

Over time, thoughts and beliefs tend to grow stronger unless something proves them to be incorrect or non-functional. When new information is introduced, we say it makes sense if it is compatible with the information we have already accepted as true. If it fits, we say it makes sense. If the information is not compatible, we say it does not make sense or that it is not correct. If it is accepted as true, it reinforces or changes the other information that we have previously accepted as true.

Our thoughts and beliefs also conform to all the above laws. If a thought or belief receives enough energy, it will turn into related actions, which will produce results that tend to reinforce the thought or the belief. In this way, we form our own reality inside of reality. When our reality is not compatible with the Universe, we suffer. When they are, we grow and prosper. When we do the right thing, we get the right result. The reason a person does not get the results they wanted is because something was wrong in the process.

We rarely question information we have already accepted as true. We rarely question the beliefs that we have accepted from our culture, society, and/or loved ones, especially if we have had them for a long time. At an early age, we learned that being a slave to anything was bad. In the history class, we learned that while the so-called slave masters were saying, "Give me liberty or give me death" that we were accepting slavery without much resistance. This type of education strongly suggests inferiority of nature and spirit.

If we believe our ancestors were slaves in slavery, we will be more likely to **attract and accept** related and similar beliefs about them. And being their descendants, we will be inclined to accept related negative thoughts about ourselves as individuals and as a people, even if we are not aware of the process. On a collective level, negative beliefs are even more powerful and influential.

Where They Come From

From like, like comes. Since there can be no action without thought, we must look for the common source of thoughts and beliefs that are producing the actions that are producing the negative results. Just because a thought is in your mind, it does not necessarily mean that it is there for the benefit of the mind it is in. it does not necessarily mean that it came from the Self. The function of thoughts and beliefs is directly related to their source.

The individual is born into a family, the family in a community, the community in a city, the city in a state and the state in a country, a country into the world and the world into the Universe. And as spirit beings in physical bodies, it is part of our nature to learn about the world and the Universe.

There are only two places that thoughts can come from. They can come from inside your spirit or from outside your spirit, from self or from other than self. Essence is Self. Our Essence is what we were at the time of our birth, even before. After that, everything else was added on.

American and European are cultures that put Africans in a unique form of human captivity called slavery and colonialism; and, have a long history of oppressing Black people even to this day. Therefore, when we evaluate our beliefs and values, we must consider their history and their source.

The thoughts and beliefs that were forced on us under slavery were meant to serve the ones that put us in slavery. A Eurocentric culture is meant to serve Europeans. Black African cultures were meant to serve the spirit of Black people. Because the culture we live in has European roots, we must learn how to separate the good thoughts from the bad thoughts. We need to understand the difference between Black African beliefs and

White European beliefs. By the law of opposites, we are this and not that.

The African American culture is European American culture painted Black. It is based on European thoughts and beliefs. It is like an African spirit with a European mind. When we look at the problems that plague Black communities, we see the same problems from north to south and coast to coast. Then we must conclude that there is a common cause. Common beliefs and thoughts produce common actions that produce common results in a common environment every time.

Living Things

Just as our living body is made of living cells, our living mind is made of living thoughts and beliefs. Thoughts and beliefs have the same basic qualities as all living things. A brief study of nature proves that life can take on forms that are beyond our imagination. The idea of this book is like a living thing. Over the years it has grown and grown and is still growing. It started out as a column for a community newspaper, grew into a pamphlet, and then into a book.

Thoughts are forms of energy. They are brought into reality or consciousness by other thoughts and beliefs. They need to be supported by other thoughts and beliefs to live. They relate to each other like birds of a feather. They work together to form living belief systems and mindsets.

The thoughts and beliefs that make up cultures and subcultures must be **cohesive or have cohesion** (the action or fact of forming a united whole). They must be **congruent** (in agreement or harmony with each other). Thoughts that are accepted as true and are not in harmony with other thoughts must be compartmentalized, quarantined, isolated, or eliminated.

Knowledge is built on knowledge. Belief is built on belief. This is how we grow from infants to adults. Therefore, the information and attitudes that we learn at an early age will have a strong influence on what we know and believe in adulthood. By the time we learn how to speak fluently, we already have a good understanding of what we are seeing and hearing. When this happens, most of the basic elements of the culture we live in have taken root.

According to what we already know and believe and the law which attracts and repels, new information will or will not make sense when it is compared to and/or integrated into the information we already have accepted as correct or incorrect according to the purpose.

The Living Mind

Each individual mind is like an **ecosystem** with all kinds of living thoughts and beliefs in it. In the mind there are billions of neural connections with thousands and thousands of thoughts being processed every day. A brief study of ecosystems shows how the various life forms relate to each other. The same basic process relates to how our minds work. It is a pattern that repeats itself over and over and permeates all of Nature.

Just as there are worlds within worlds, there are thoughts inside of thoughts and beliefs inside of beliefs. The process can be compared to an egg or a seed. In time, a seed can grow into a whole tree; an egg into a whole chicken or a human being depending on what type of egg or seed it is.

A Symbiotic Relationship

We have an interdependent relationship with our thoughts and beliefs. They are a part of what we are. We see ourselves as being one with them. We can feel that they are a vital part of who we are. If our thoughts and beliefs are threatened, we tend to feel as if we are being attacked. This often leads to arguments and strong negative feelings towards those who do not understand, disagree, or call our ideas and beliefs stupid.

An attack on our thoughts and beliefs is an attack on our ego. Sometimes, we are willing to fight and even die for what we believe if the feeling is strong enough. Therefore, we tend to cling to what we have already accepted as true and/or what the collective mind or culture accepts as true.

The Purpose of Thoughts

In Nature, birds must learn how to fly. Predators must learn how to hunt. Prey animals must learn how to escape predators. Their learning and their skills must conform to their nature if they are going to continue to exist in their environment. Their Nature is directly related to their genetic and culture and social histories.

By Nature, the ultimate purpose of thoughts, beliefs, knowledge, and learning are to assist that which we were born with, our Essence. Some people call it the soul. Therefore, the purpose of learning and knowledge is to assist our spirit in the physical world and the spiritual or nonphysical world as well.

Because of the history of Euro-American culture as it relates to the American African, it is necessary for us to educate or re-educate ourselves particularly in the areas that relate to our culture, history, identity, and spirituality. The thoughts that were implanted in us about us under slavery were meant to benefit the ones that put us in slavery.

Therefore, if our thoughts and beliefs do not bring us the results that help us, that generate peace and harmony among us, we must ask, how did we come to accept the beliefs and values that form our current collective state of mind and culture? Who benefits from our pain and suffering?

If what you did, did not benefit you, then what you did was what someone else wanted you to do.

The fact that we call our ancestors slaves and the confusion in the language about the words slave and slavery is testimony to the fact that we have been mis-educated about our history and our natural identity. The following is a quote from Carter G. Woodson, the "Father of Black History."

The same educational process which inspires and stimulates the oppressor with the thought that he is everything and has accomplished everything worthwhile, depresses and crushes at the same time the spark of genius in the Negro by making him feel

*that his race does not amount to much and never will
measure up to the standards of other peoples. pg. xiii*

The Miseducation of the Negro,1933
Carter G. Woodson,

And it is still true to this day. As we begin and continue to educate ourselves about ourselves, we should leave no stone unturned. We should walk a mile in our ancestors' shoes. We should not accept what **they** tell us at face value. We should allow the information we have accepted as true and new information to be tested and re-tested. With the power of the internet and the library, there is no subject that we cannot study.

The Science of Thought

As thoughts and beliefs function according to universal laws and order, there is a science to it. For the most part, we have been educated in the areas of how to get a good job, in the various areas of technology, but not in the science of life or how to live in a way where we can experience "heaven on Earth". We have not been educated in the science of the spirit world or the nonphysical.

Therefore, it is necessary for us to educate ourselves to achieve this goal. Achieving this goal is not dependent on money, material possession, or a particular circumstance. It is dependent on understanding the laws mentioned above and understanding how thoughts and beliefs work. Are our thoughts and beliefs producing the results we want?

Good Thoughts, Bad Thoughts

This process is better illustrated in the lyrics of a song by The Funkadelic, produced by George Clinton, from the album Standing on the Verge of Getting it On, called "Good Thoughts, Bad Thoughts":

Travel like a king.

Listen to the inner voice.

A higher wisdom is at work for you.

Conquering the stumbling blocks comes easier when the conqueror is in tune with the infinite.

Every ending is a new beginning.

Life is an endless unfoldment.

Change your mind, and you change your relation to time.

You can find the answer.

The solution lies within the problem.

The answer is in every question.

Dig it?

An attitude is all you need to rise and walk away.

Inspire yourself. Your life is yours. It fits you like your skin.

The oak sleeps in the acorn.

The giant sequoia tree sleeps in its tiny seed.

The bird waits in the egg.

God waits for his unfoldment in man.

PRINCIPLES & ISSUES
Rules of Reality and Thought

Fly on children. Play on.

You gravitate to that which you secretly love most.

You meet in life the exact reproduction of your own thoughts.

There is no chance, coincidence or accident in a world ruled by law and divine order.

You rise as high as your dominant aspiration.

You descend to the level of your lowest concept of yourself.

Free your mind and your ass will follow.

The infinite intelligence within you knows the answers.

Its nature is to respond to your thoughts.

Be careful of the thought-seeds you plant in the garden of your mind. For seeds grow after their kind.

Play on children.

Every thought felt as true or allowed to be accepted as true by your conscious mind takes roots in your subconscious, blossoms sooner or later into an act, and bears its own fruit.

Good thoughts bring forth good fruit.

Bullshit thoughts rot your meat.

Think right, and you can fly.

The kingdom of heaven is within.

Free your mind and your ass will follow.

Play on children. Sing on lady.

The belief that our ancestors were slaves is a bad seed. If we accept it as true, we can only get bad results from it. All of the above laws apply to everything we do every day. They apply to what we do as individuals as well as to what we do as a people. They apply to what we do in private as well as to all of our social interactions.

Why We Believe Our Ancestors Were Slaves

Maybe we believe it because we look at our history through the eyes of the people who captured, tortured, rewarded, and then educated us. Maybe we believe it because almost everyone else believes it. Is it because every time we see a documentary or a movie about slavery, we see Black African people submitting to inhuman conditions like "slaves?" Is it because they say it over and over, "the slaves", "the slaves", "the slaves?" They seem to run it in the ground.

Maybe we believe it because we have problems dealing with that part of our history. For many of us, the images and thoughts of slavery are very painful because we naturally tend to identify with our ancestors. The pain of it automatically prompts us to avoid looking at and thinking about what we experienced under slavery. By avoiding it, we have not taken a deeper look at this issue.

But why should we expect those who have a Euro-centric point of view to understand or to tell us the truth about the history of Africans in America and Africa? And why should we accept what they say at face value without question?

The Reverse Psychology

How many times have we heard that we should be proud of our history? How can we be proud of being slaves; which is not the same as saying that we can be proud of how we operated under slavery?

How can we be proud of being savages and being a backward people in Africa? Relative to the time and environment, African people were no more backward than any other people, even the Europeans living in cities and towns. How can we be proud of (or even make a good judgment of) something of which we have little knowledge?

This is a contradiction in logic. If we cannot take pride in being slaves (*according to the original definition*), how can we take pride in being the descendants of slaves and savages? How can we be proud of who we are? We tell our children and ourselves to be proud of our history and then treat it as if it began in America under the despotism of the American government.

As a result, only a relatively few Black people have any interest in studying anything that relates to the origin and cultures of Black people. In effect, it is a form of forced self-rejection. Believing that our ancestors were slaves allows us to believe that we are now free when the opposite may be more correct. If we believe we are free, we will see no need to try to get free.

The reverse psychology is that it looks like "they" are telling us to do one thing; but what is being taught prompts us to do the opposite. It looks like we are being encouraged to study our own history, then it is treated as if it is almost irrelevant by giving us very little of it. And, what little we do get is distorted. What we do get does not encourage us to learn more about African people, culture, philosophy, or history. Our education has not motivated most individuals to do the things that help us to develop our communities and families or to have much hope for our future. Reverse psychology, negative **propaganda**, lies, and confusion are relatives of the same family. They are the cornerstone of slavery.

Being Free

Having rights to do particular things is not the same as being free. Prisoners have rights. Dr. Martin Luther King recognized the fact that we are not free in his 1963 "*I Have A Dream*" *speech*, when he said "*...But one hundred years later, the Negro still is not free.*"[3] If we are not free, then what does freedom mean? What would it mean if we were free?

Being free means that we are free to be ourselves. In order to be ourselves, we must understand our God given true identity as a people and as individuals of that people. In order to understand our true identity, we must understand where we came from, our history, and our natural cultures.

The Truth Is

However, the truth is that Black African people captured under slavery acted no differently than any other people would have under the same conditions. The truth is that slavery was very different from any other form of human servitude before it. The truth is that Africans in America under slavery resisted and forced the Government to change the conditions of slavery and to come up with the Emancipation Proclamation.

[1] As A Man Thinketh "Thought & Character" by James Allen, (ISBN: 0-88029-785-9, 1992) p.2

[2] Brainwashed, Challenging the Myth of Black Inferiority by Tom Burrell, (ISBN: 978-1-4019-25925,) p.ix

[3] Martin Luther King Jr. I Have A Dream, ed by James M. Washington (ISBN: 0-06-250552-1) p.102

www.ingramcontent.com/pod-product-compliance
Lightning Source LLC
Chambersburg PA
CBHW070048070426
42449CB00012BA/3186